THE BEST OF
BALTIMORE BEAUTIES PART II

More Patterns for Album Blocks

Elly Sienkiewicz

C&T PUBLISHING

© 2002 by Elly Sienkiewicz
Editor: Cyndy Lyle Rymer
Technical Editor: Karyn Hoyt-Culp
Copyeditor/Proofreader: Laura Reinstatler/Emily Hopkins
Cover Designer: Kristen Yenche
Design Director/Book Designer: Kristen Yenche and Tim Manibusan
Illustrator: Jeffrey Carillo
Production Assistant: Tim Manibusan
Photography: Sharon Risedorph unless otherwise noted
Published by C&T Publishing, Inc., P.O. Box 1456, Lafayette,
California 94549

Front cover: "Theorem Style Urn of Fruit", New Pattern #10
Back cover: "Square Wreath of Embroidered Flowers", New Pattern #8,
"Baltimore Basket of Roses", New Pattern #6, "Heart Wreath of Acorns",
New Pattern #2

Library of Congress Cataloging-in-Publication Data

Sienkiewicz, Elly.
  The best of Baltimore beauties : 95 patterns for album blocks and
borders / Elly Sienkiewicz.
      p. cm.
Includes index.
   ISBN 1-57120-149-1 (paper trade)
   1. Appliqué—Patterns. 2. Album quilts—Maryland—Baltimore.
   3. Patchwork—Patterns. I. Title.
   TT779 .S5424 1999
   746.46'041—dc21
                              99-050545

Published by C&T Publishing, Inc.
P.O. Box 1456
Lafayette, California 94549

Printed in China
10 9 8 7 6 5 4 3 2 1

Contents

Lyre Floral Fruit Album Wreath Birds Basket Border Heart

Papercut Vase Music Cornucopia House Ship Frame Tree Fleur-De-Lis

GLOSSARY 9

PREFACE 11

INTRODUCTION 16

BALTIMORE ALBUM QUILTS

PATTERN 1   Fleur-de-Lis Medallion I 19

PATTERN 2   Fleur-de-Lis II 20

PATTERN 4   Betty Alderman's Scherenschnitte 21

PATTERN 5   Sylvia's Wycinanki 22

PATTERN 6   Hearts and Swans I and II 23

PATTERN 7   Rose of Sharon II 24

PATTERN 8   Folk Art Flower Wheel 25

PATTERN 10   Red Vases and Red Flowers 26

PATTERN 11   Victorian Favorite 27

PATTERN 14   Fleur-de-Lis with Rosebuds IV 28

PATTERN 15   Grapevine Wreath II 29

PATTERN 16   Strawberry Wreath II 30

PATTERN 18   Circular Sprays of Flowers 31

PATTERN 21   Fleur-de-Lis Medallion II 32

PATTERN 24   Rose Cornucopias 34

PATTERN 30   Vase with Fruits and Flowers 36

PATTERN 41   Victorian Basket of Flowers IV 38

PATTERN 42   Victorian Basket V with Fruits and Flowers 42

PATTERN 44   Scalloped Epergne of Fruit 46

Contents *(continued)*

BALTIMORE BEAUTIES AND BEYOND, Volume II

PATTERN 1	Hans Christian Andersen's Danish Hearts	◈♥	50
PATTERN 7	Heart Medallion Frame	♥◻	51
PATTERN 8	Goose Girl Milking	⮞♣	53
PATTERN 9	Hearts and Hands in a Feather Wreath	♥♣	54
PATTERN 12	Wreaths of Hearts I and II	◯♥	56
PATTERN 13	Bird in a Fruit Wreath	◯◓⮞	58
PATTERN 15	Goose Girl	⮞🌳♣	62
PATTERN 16	Waterfowling	⮞♣	66
PATTERN 17	Tropical Boating	⮞♣🌳	70
PATTERN 21	The Peony Border	✉	74

DIMENSIONAL APPLIQUÉ

PATTERN 7	Rick Rack Roses	◯♣♥	76
PATTERN 8	Flower-Wreathed Heart II	◯♥♣	78
PATTERN 9	Lovely Lane's Grapevine Wreath	◯◓	80
PATTERN 11	Basket of Quarter Roses and Buds	🧺♣	82
PATTERN 12	Unadorned Victorian Basket of Flowers	🧺♣	84
PATTERN 14	Folk Art Basket of Flowers	🧺♣	86
PATTERN 15	Apples in the Late Afternoon	🧺◓	90
PATTERN 16	Ivy Basket with Bow	🧺	94
PATTERN 17	Jeannie's Iris, Pansy, and Pleated Flowers Basket	🧺♣	98
PATTERN 18	Regal Bird Amidst the Roses	⮞♣🧺	102
PATTERN 21	Baltimore Bouquet	♣	106
PATTERN 27	Pedestal Basket with Handle	🧺	110
PATTERN 28	Annie Tuley's Pleated Basket	🧺	110
PATTERN 33	Kaye's Ribbon Basket	🧺	111
PATTERN 32	Ribbonwork Basket for Broderie Perse Blooms	🧺	111
Two Borders		✉	112, 121
Color Section			113–120